Icy Irene's Adventure in an Igloo

Making Alliteration Fun For All Types!

Written by
Nicky Gaymer-Jones

Illustrated by
Kaelin Twede

ISBN: 978-1-964411-08-8 (paperback)

Front cover image and book design by Amber Leigh Luecke

Printed in the United States of America

First printing edition 2024

Dedicated to all of the great teachers
who believe in their students.

Irene lives in an igloo in Antarctica.
She is surrounded by ice!

1

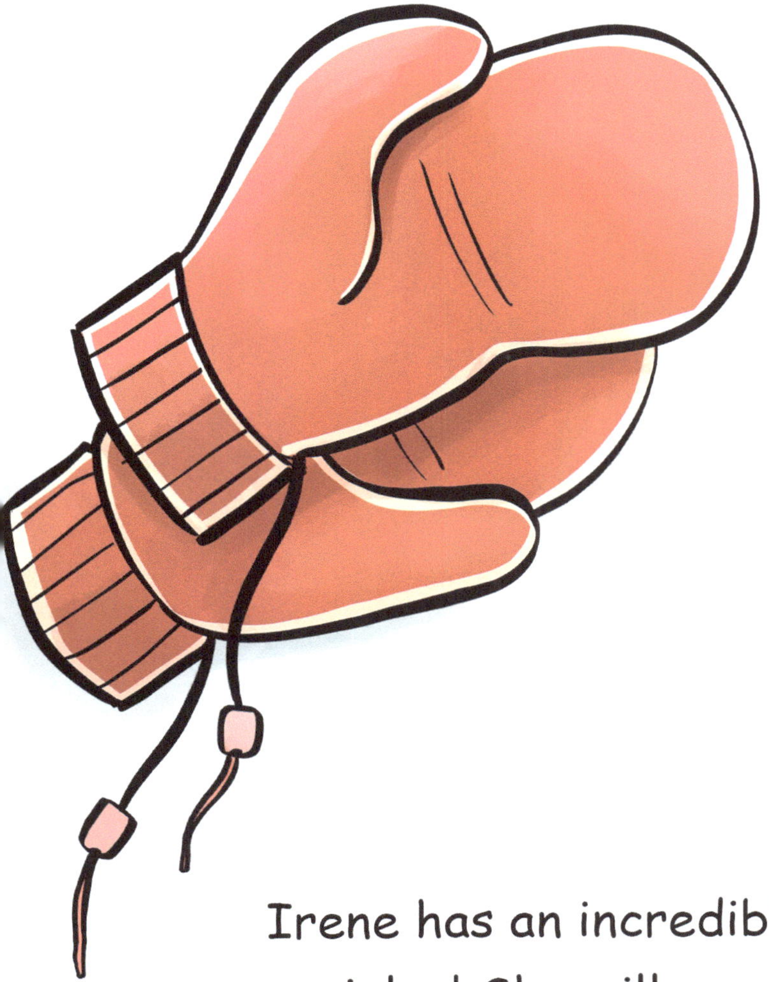

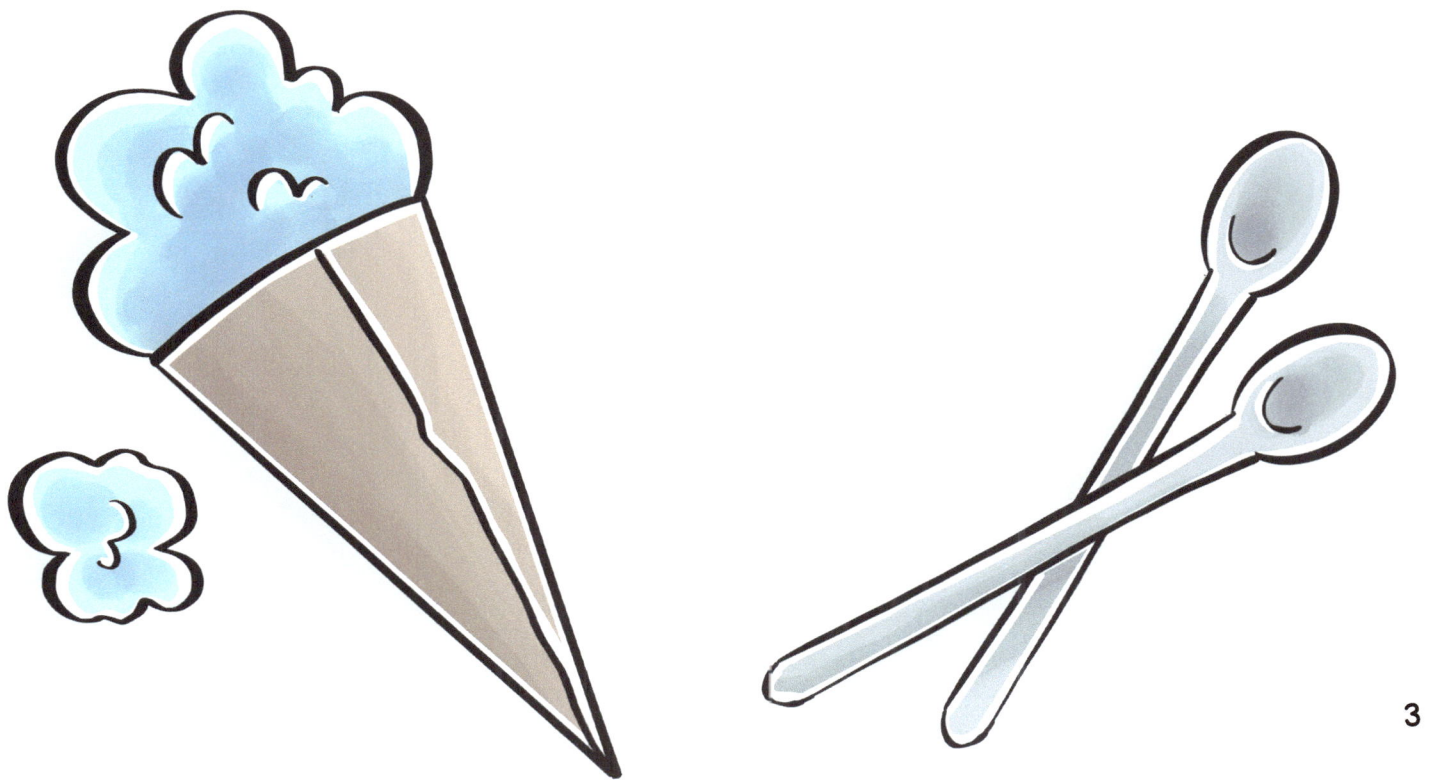

Irene has an incredible idea to improve her
igloo! She will carve ice with an icicle
to make lots of ice furniture for her igloo.

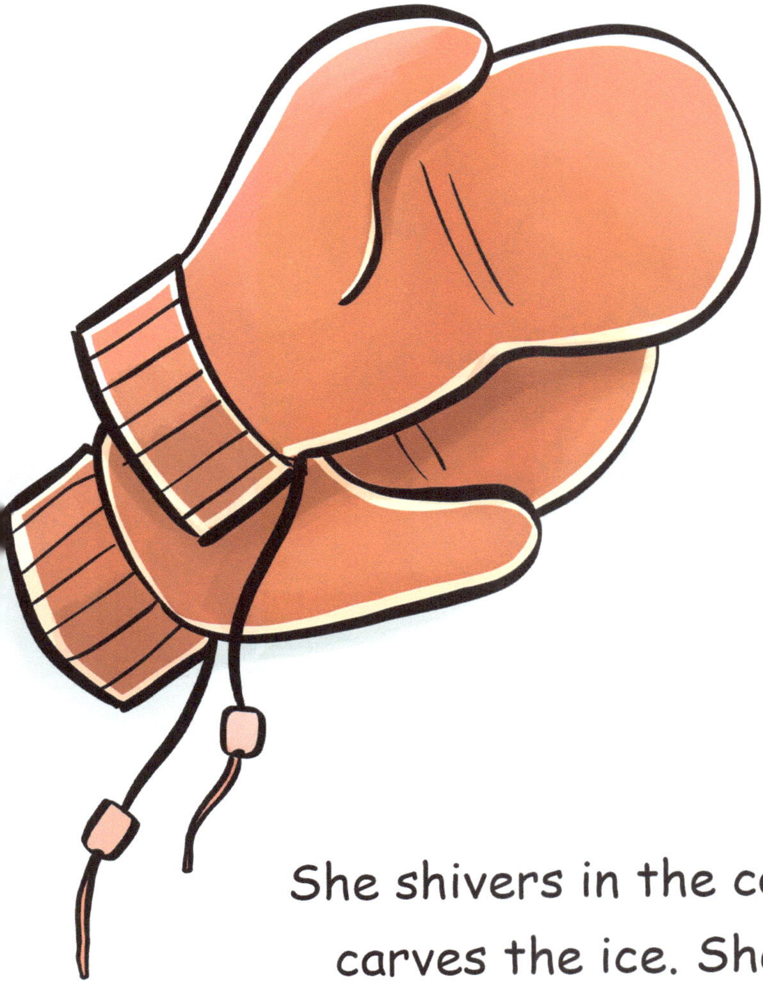

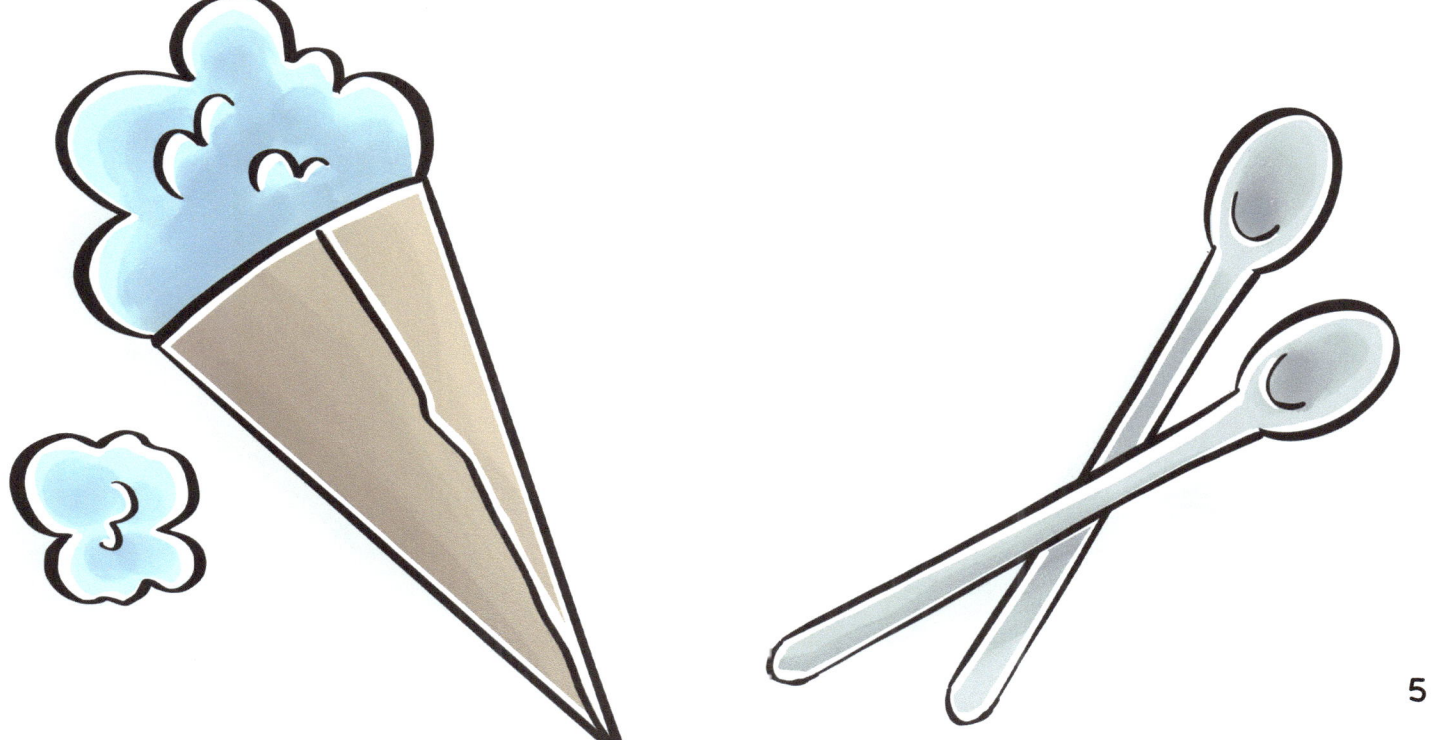

She shivers in the cold. Inch-by-inch, she
carves the ice. She makes many items
for her igloo, and they look very icy.
"What else should I do?"

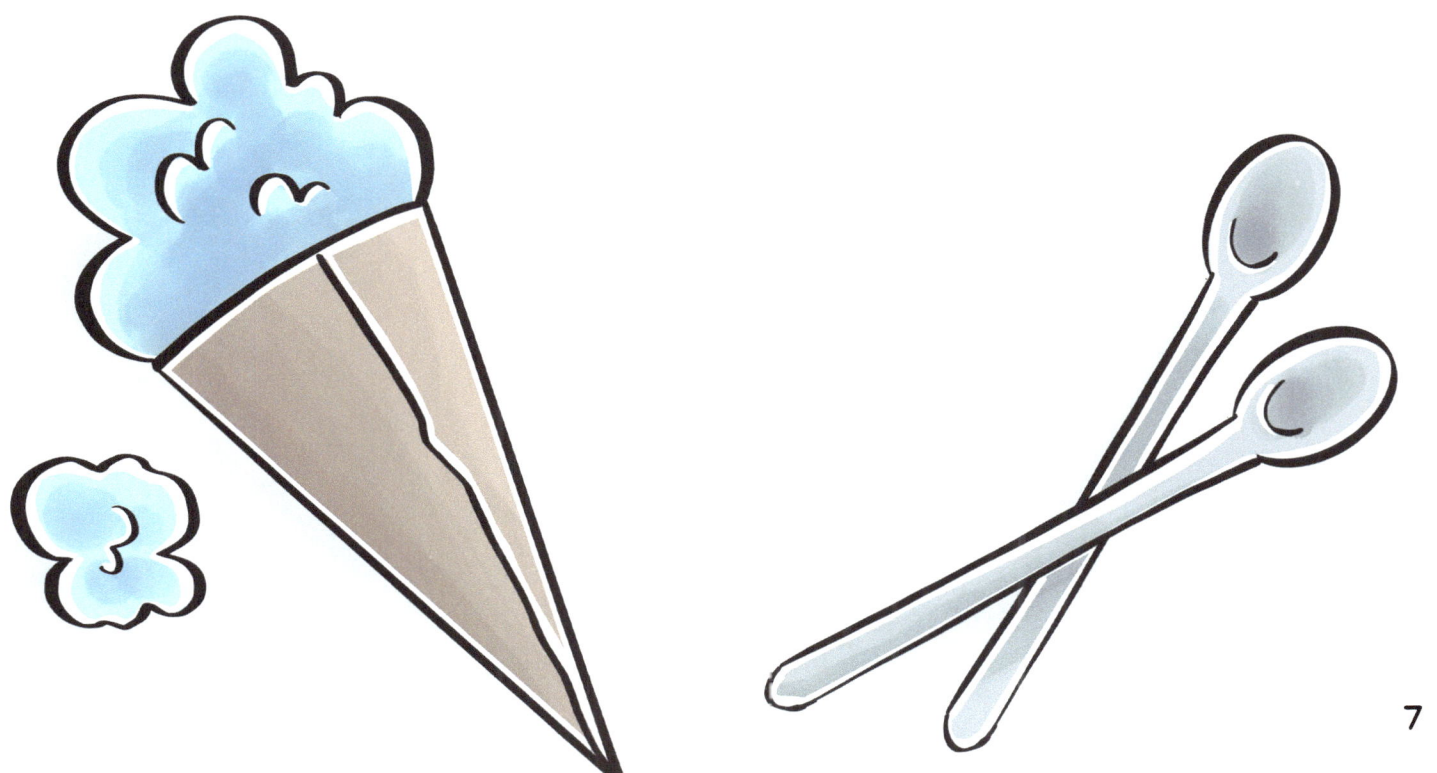

Irene crawls out of her igloo and
sees an ice cream stand.
"Mmm! I love ice cream!"

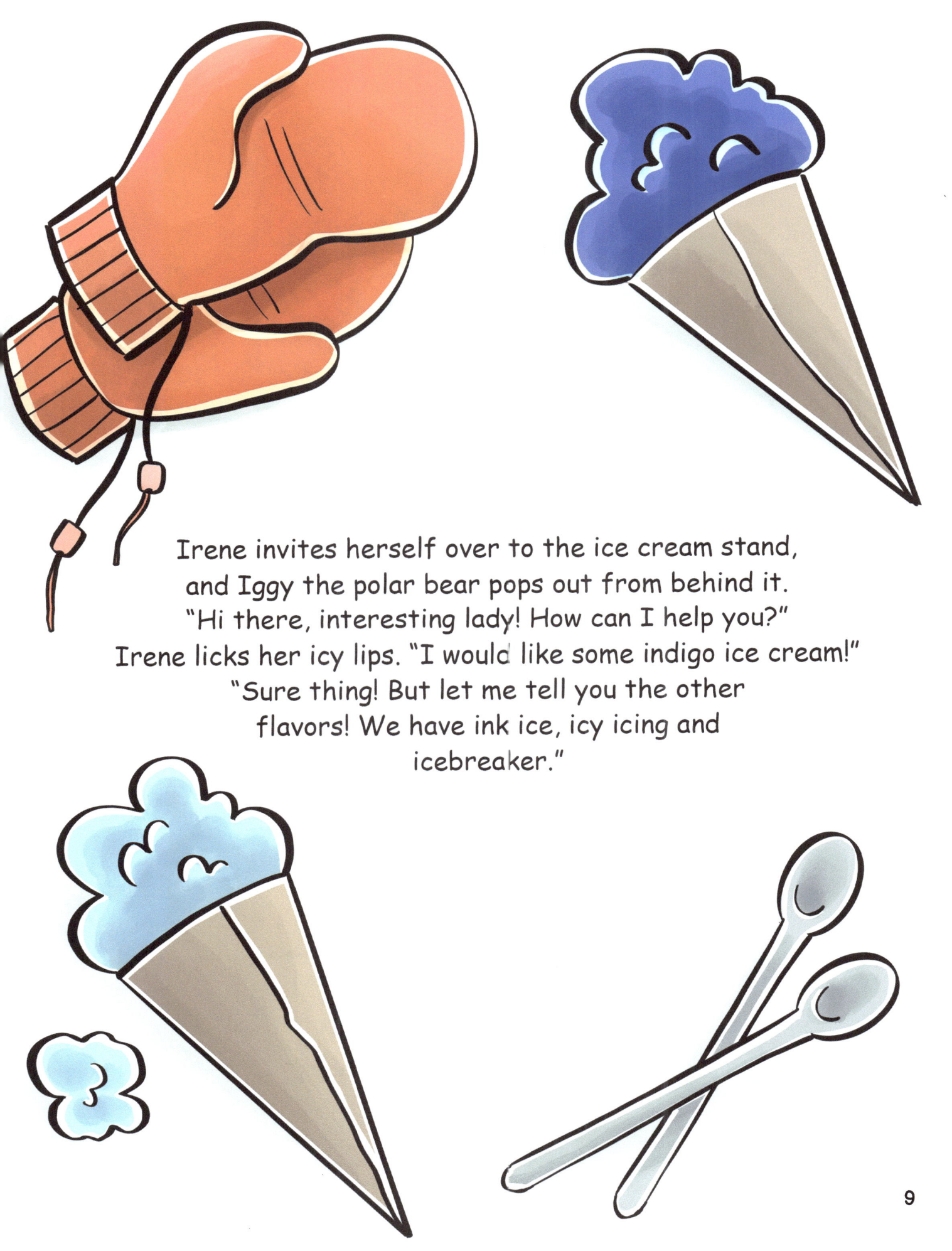

Irene invites herself over to the ice cream stand,
and Iggy the polar bear pops out from behind it.
"Hi there, interesting lady! How can I help you?"
Irene licks her icy lips. "I would like some indigo ice cream!"
"Sure thing! But let me tell you the other
flavors! We have ink ice, icy icing and
icebreaker."

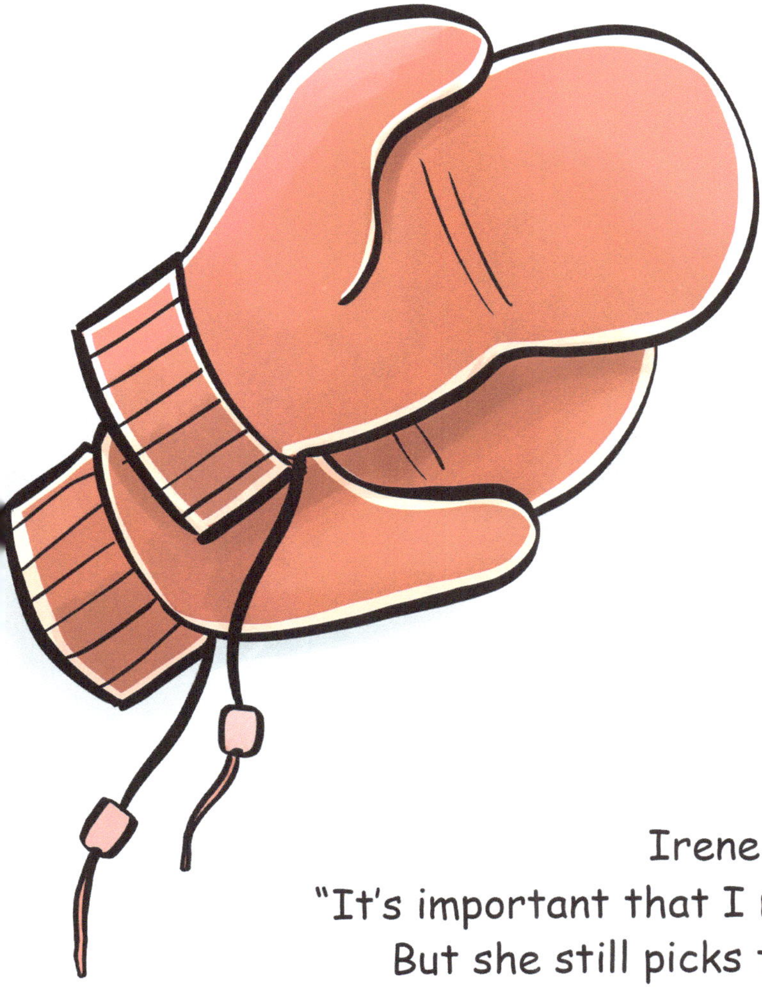

Irene thinks,
"It's important that I make the best decision."
But she still picks the indigo ice cream.
Iggy hands Irene the ice cream. "Here you go!"

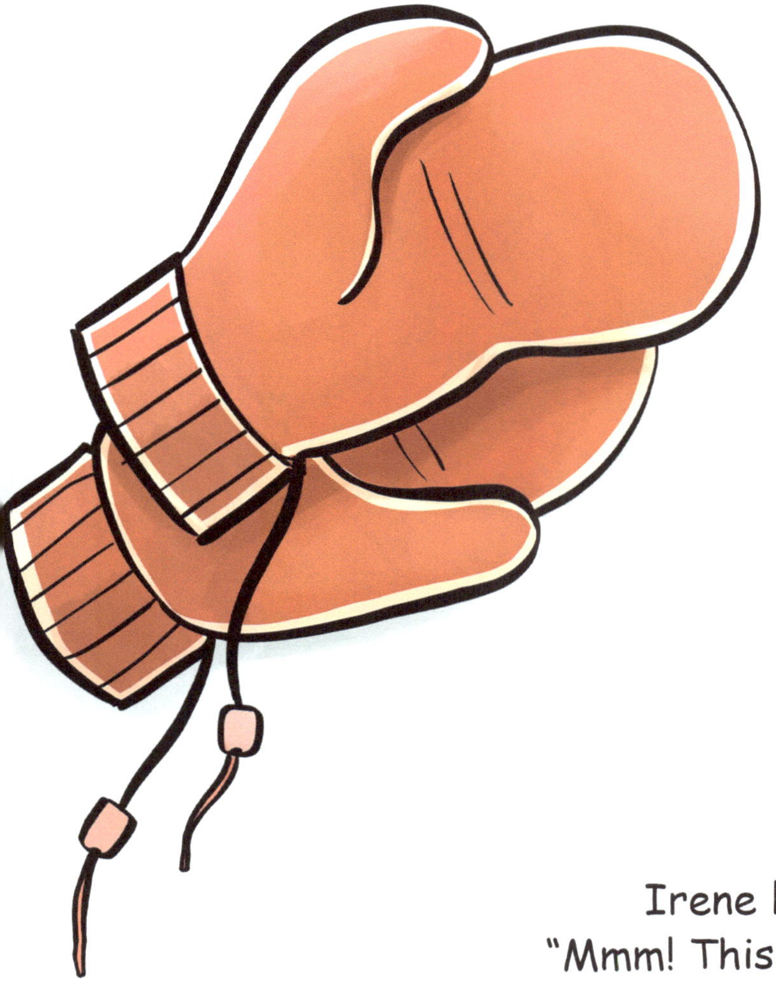

Irene licks it.
"Mmm! This is delicious!
Now, back to making things for my igloo."

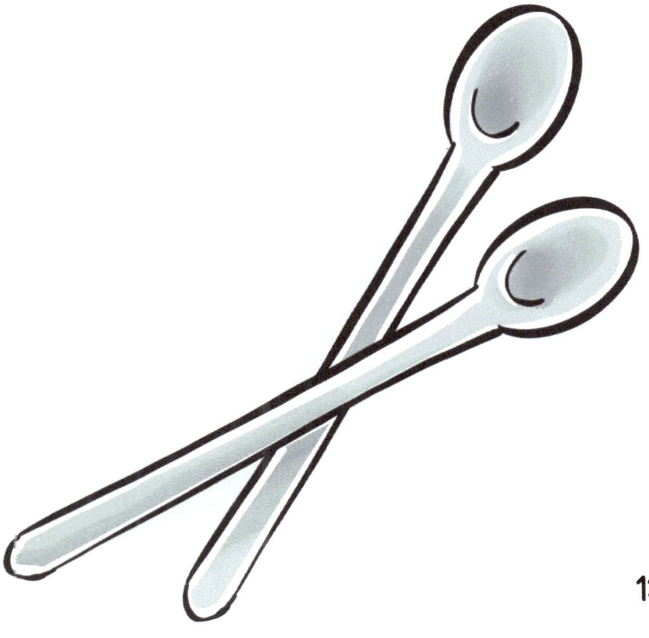

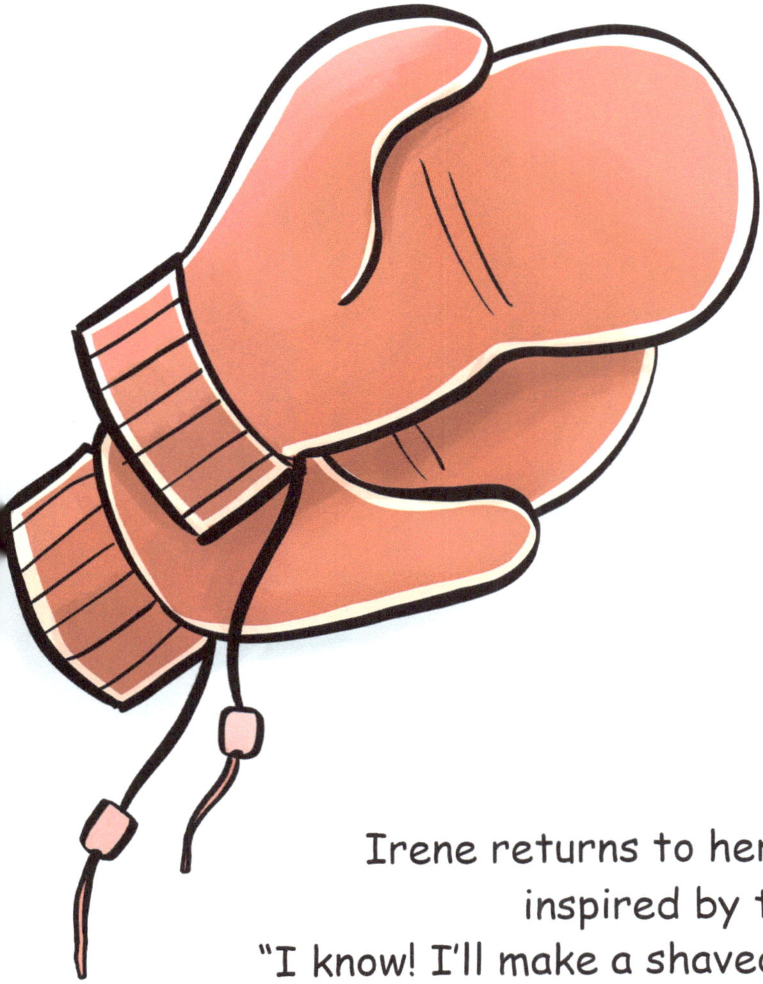

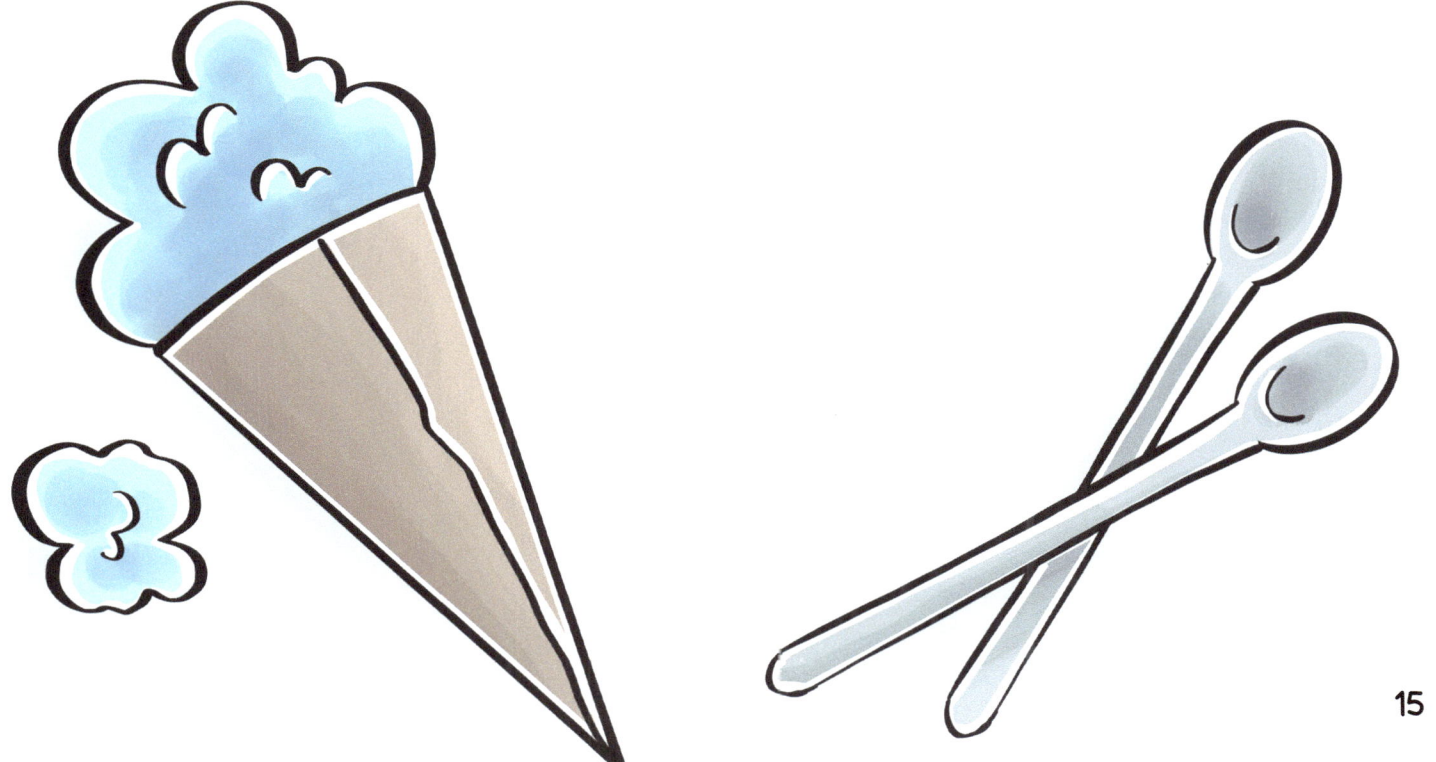

Irene returns to her igloo and is suddenly
inspired by the ice cream.
"I know! I'll make a shaved ice stand inside my igloo!"
Irene has lots of colored syrup in her igloo and, of course,
lots of ice. But she still needs cones!

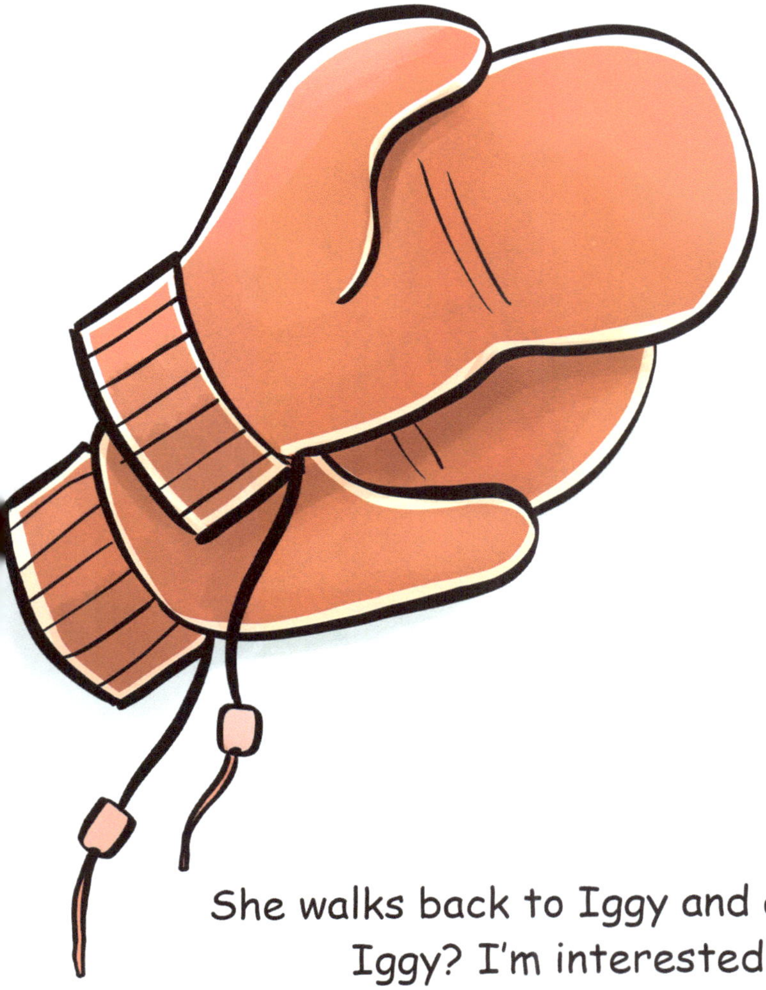

She walks back to Iggy and asks, "Can I have some cones, Iggy? I'm interested in making shaved ice."
Iggy gives her some icy cones.

"Thank you!" she says, and crawls back into her igloo to make incredible ice flavors.

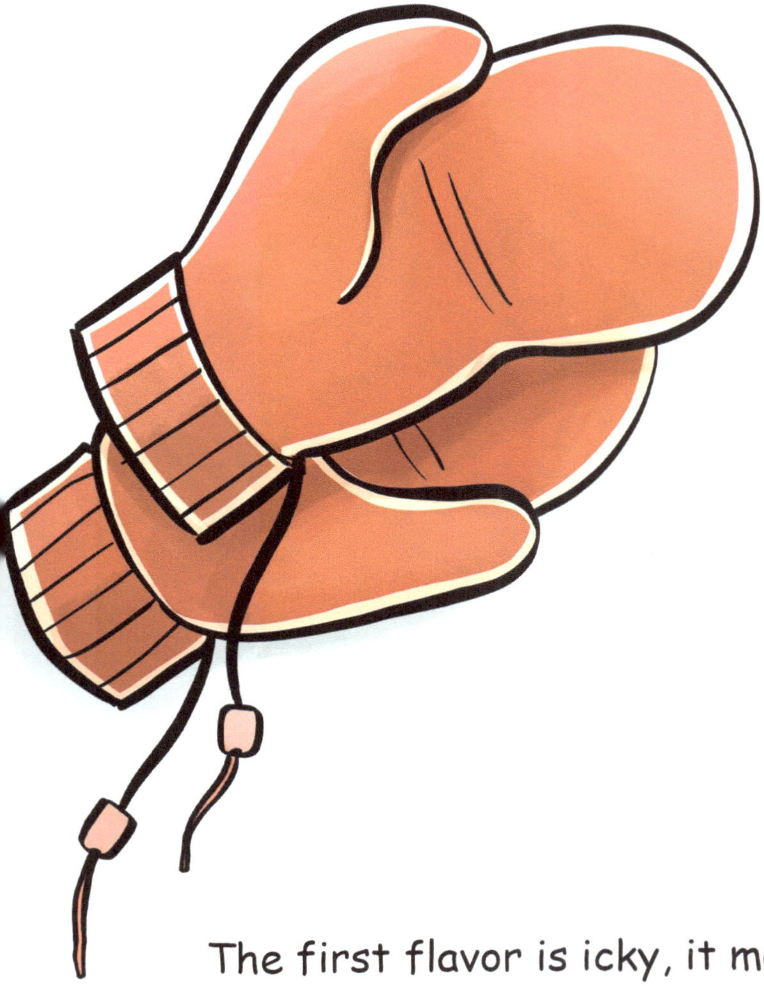

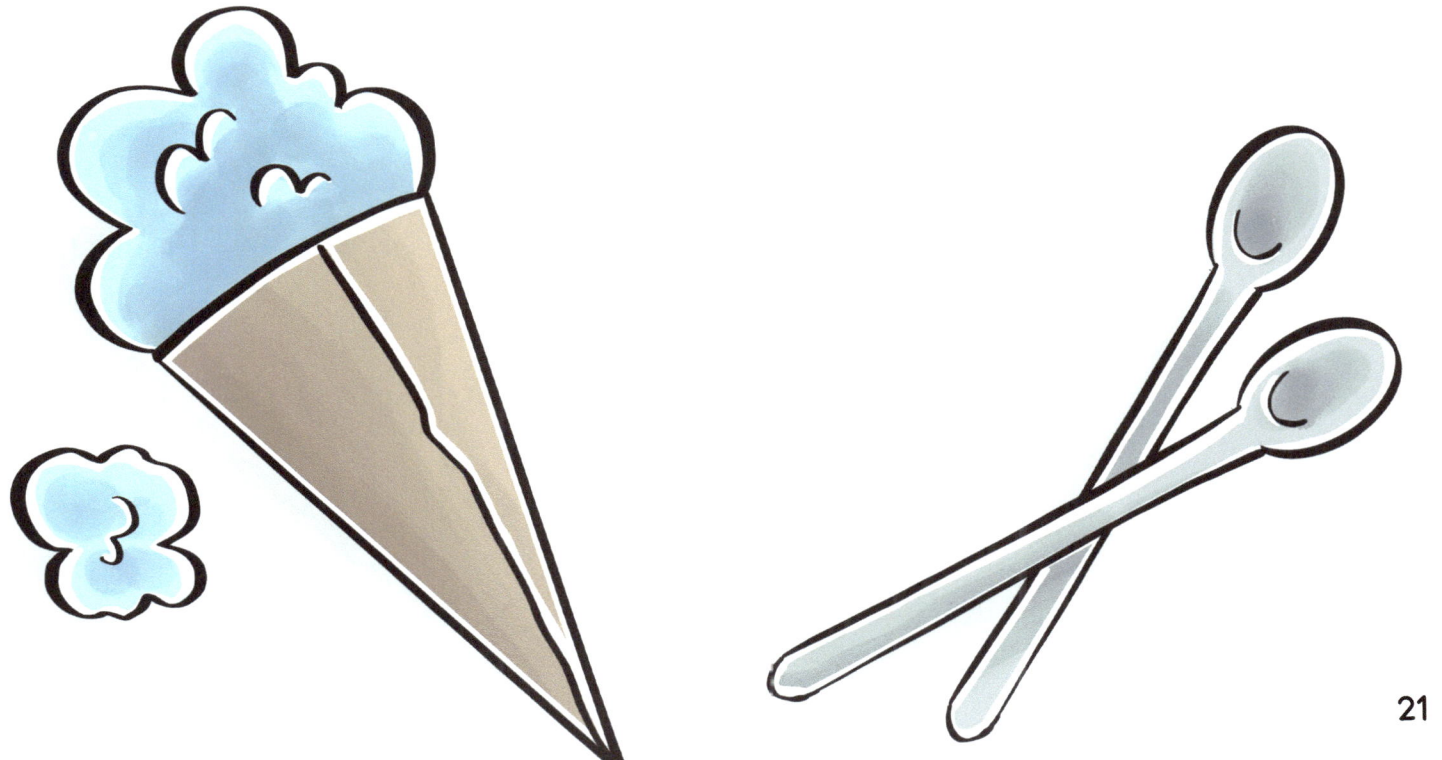

The first flavor is icky, it makes her ill. The second one is iffy, it made her irritated. The third showed improvement, it was ideal!

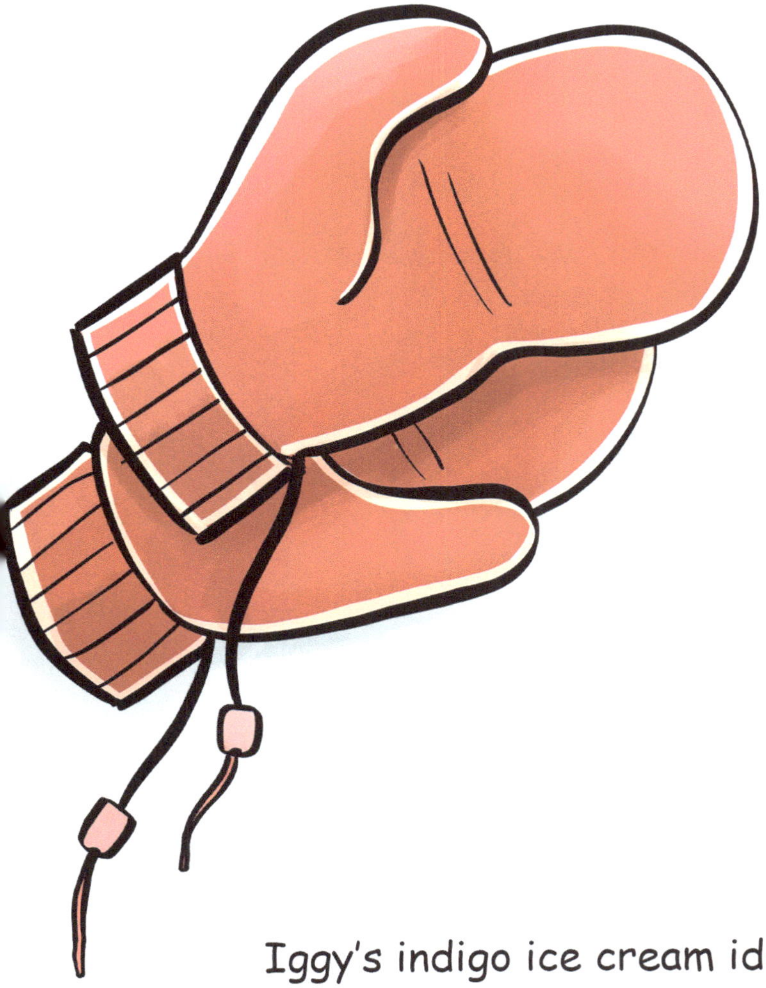

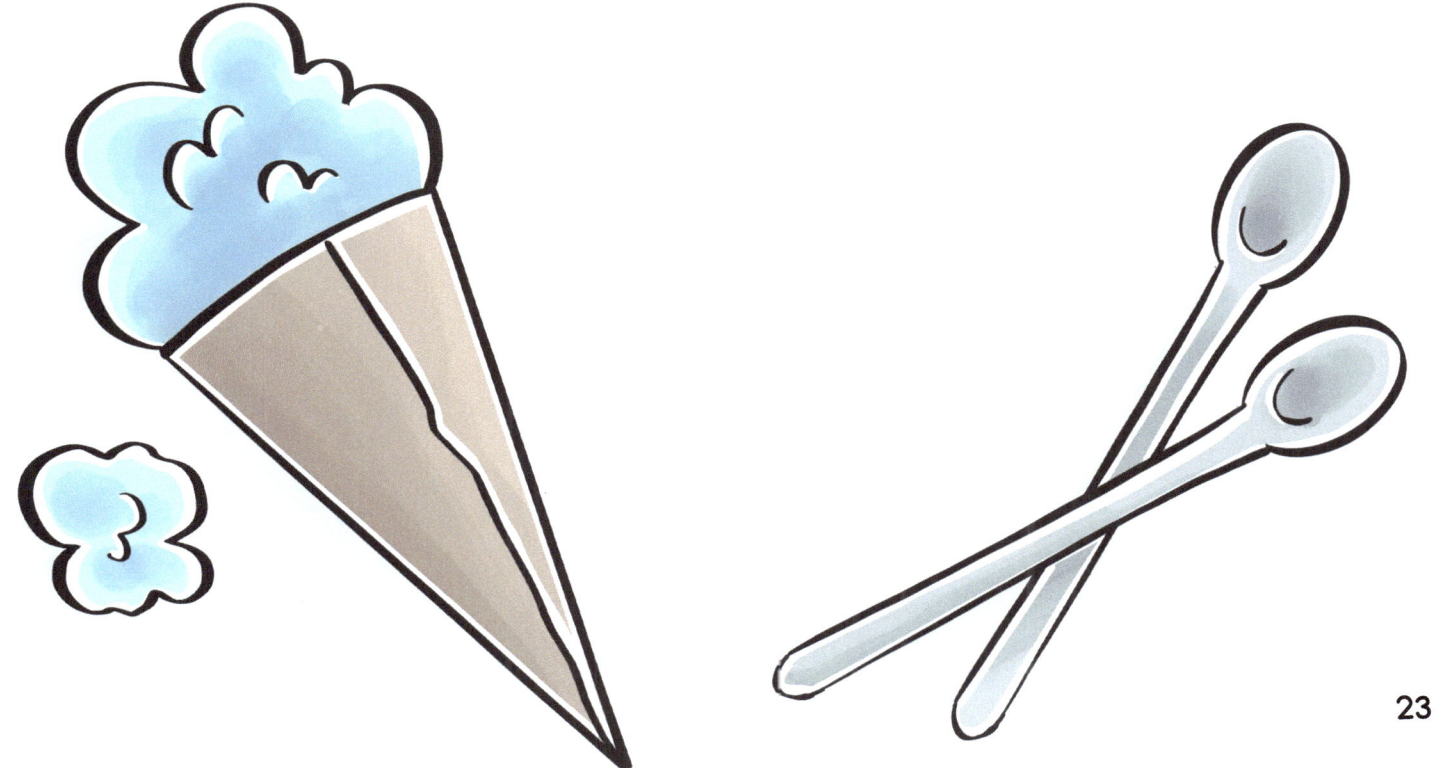

Iggy's indigo ice cream idea was iconic. Irene was so inspired her imagination itches to create her own improved indigo ice cream!

Discover the Wonders of Alliteration:
A Complete Collection from A to Z!

Dive into a world of wonder and learning with the "Alliteration Fun for All Types" Complete Collection, where each amusing story is dedicated to a specific letter of the alphabet.

From adventurous ants to zany zebras, these captivating tales are designed to engage and empower readers of all types, including those with dyslexia or other learning differences.

This collection of fun stories weaves rhythm, rhyming, and the magic of alliteration to foster a love of reading and promote inclusivity in storytelling.

Whether you're seeking an educational adventure, or inspiring a new reader, this collection promises to captivate young minds and instill a lifelong love for the magic of words.

To learn more visit Nickysbooks.com

If you enjoyed this book, please leave a review on Amazon and help new readers discover Nicky's books.
Thank you.

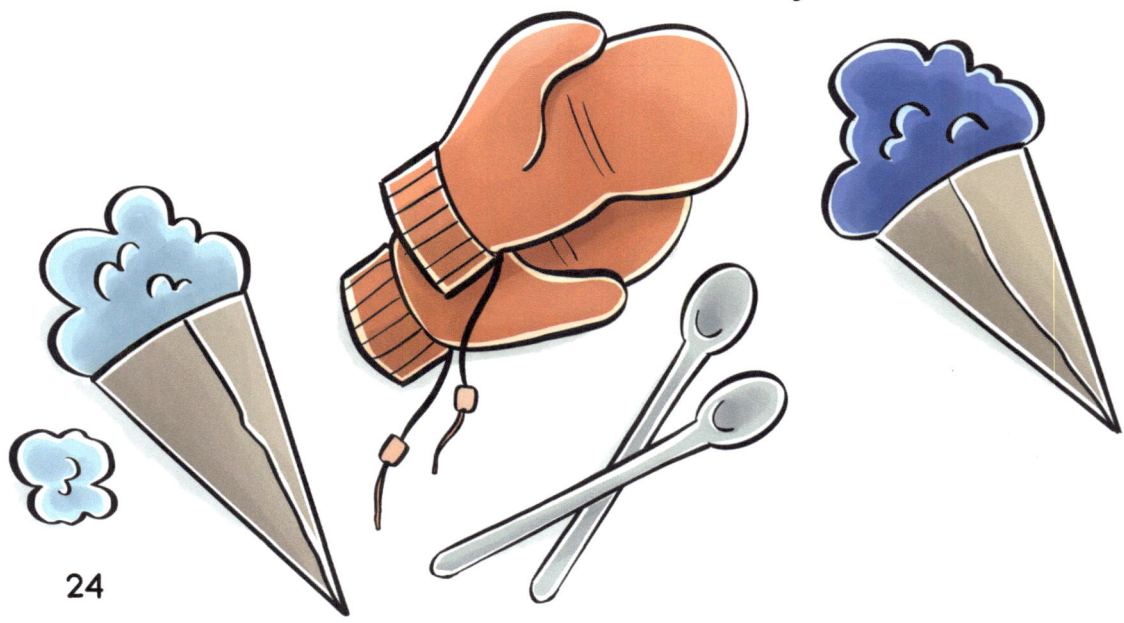

24